This special edition of

RESULTS

There's No Such Word as Can't

Is provided to you courtesy of

2 Bethesda Metro Center, Suite 1200
Bethesda, MD 20814

1-877-4-HANGER
1-877-442-6437

www.Hanger.com

I

The people at Hanger want you to know that we support your dreams. Our most important goal is to help you achieve your highest potential.

Hanger Prosthetics & Orthotics is therefore delighted to present you with this book as a complimentary gift. Its motivational and results-based strategies are designed to assist you in your life challenge, whatever it may be. We believe this book will help you to focus on success, whether that means climbing a step or climbing a mountain. We hope the message in this book puts you firmly on the road to success and obtaining RESULTS.

RESULTS

There's No Such Word as Can't

by

Dale Berry

R E S U L T S

There's No Such Word as Can't

Dale Berry

Printed in the United States of America

ISBN: 1-891231-34-0

Library of Congress Catalog Control Number: 00-192777

Word Association Publishers
205 Fifth Avenue
Tarentum, Pennsylvania 15084
800-827-7903
www.wordassociation.com

To my father

Murray

Who taught me integrity, honor and there is no such word as can't.

To my grandfather,

Dan Allen

Who taught me friendship and how to think outside the box.

To my sons,

Mitchell and Tyler

Who taught me to love life everyday.

And to my wife,

Jean

Who taught me how to love.

Acknowledgments

This book never would have been possible without the hundreds of individuals that I have had the pleasure of providing prosthetic care for over the past 20 years. Each one has shared their hardship, victory, inspiration and a part of their lives that has had a profound impact on my life. I thank each and every patient I have worked with for giving me your trust and confidence and allowing me to design and fit your prosthesis.

I owe a special thanks to my older brother Daniel Berry. His insight and editorial input in the writing of this book were invaluable. I seems that no matter how much I age, there is always a benefit in having an older brother to turn to. I thank my friend and Pastor, Keith Magnuson, his friendship and prayers are always a comfort. I want to recognize my editor Tom Costello, his patience, skill and expertise were a significant contribution to this book. To Ian Gamson, I offer my deepest appreciation for his encouragement and support. He has shown me the value, power and grace of being truly authentic; Ian defines a mentor and a gentleman. I thank my wife Jean for providing the understanding, confidence and assistance to make this book a reality. I thank her for listening to my stories, teaching me how to love, showing me how to dream and most importantly, I thank Jean for being my partner in building our future.

Introduction

When I was a small boy, my father used to say to me, "There is no such word as can't." Whenever I got frustrated or experienced challenge, I would tell my father, "I can't do it, it's too hard." And Dad would always disagree. I was confused for years; after all, the word can't is in the dictionary. But showing my dad the dictionary was to no avail. Dad always stuck to his premise. "It doesn't matter what it says in a book," was his standard reply. "In life, there's no such word as can't."

Little did I know how well his simple message would prepare me for my chosen career. As a certified prosthetist, I design and fit artificial limbs, or prostheses, for individuals who have experienced the trauma of amputation. From the first day of my residency, I have witnessed the power of the human spirit as patients in my care overcome the challenge of amputation to literally get back on their feet again. I have seen individuals who have lost one, two, three, and even four limbs refuse to be defeated by the challenge of amputation. Somehow they find it within themselves to overcome the challenges and create a meaningful and productive life.

Early in my residency I evaluated a young man about my own age who had undergone double amputation surgery--one leg removed above the knee and the other just below the knee--due to a motorcycle accident. During the evaluation I sought to determine his expectations with regard to prosthetic rehabilitation, and I asked him if he had any special goals. Without missing a beat, he responded, "I want to be able to ride a motorcycle." Such a goal, even if it could be realized after radical amputation, would take a tremendous amount of work and determination from the patient. I had never heard of a double amputee who was capable of riding a motorcycle, and I doubted whether I was capable of designing such sophisticated prostheses. I patiently explained that the extent of the amputations and the limitations of technology pointed to a less ambitious goal for now and that the motorcycle goal should be saved for a little later on. But he cut me off. "The name of the game is RESULTS," he asserted. "You asked what I wanted and I gave you my answer. Now you do your job and I'll do mine." At first I attributed his emotional response to frustration over his amputations. However, the more he shared his dream of getting back on a motorcycle and feeling the freedom of the open road, the more I realized he was right. My job was--and remains to this day--to deliver RESULTS, nothing more, nothing less.

No matter how good the practitioner, no matter how well-designed the prosthesis, no matter how credible the goal or expectation, the only thing that really matters is that I deliver the RESULTS my patients demand so that they in turn can achieve their goal. What good would it be if a patient almost learned to walk or was almost able to stand up? Almost is not an acceptable outcome. RESULTS are what matter, and RESULTS are the only outcome my patients will accept.

To this day, I think of that young man's response every time I interact with a patient. More importantly, that experience made me realize that a RESULTS-oriented philosophy could be applied to many aspects of my personal and professional life. After all, whenever I take on a new challenge or attempt to overcome an obstacle, RESULTS are really what I am after. Without RESULTS, a lot of energy is uselessly expended and many experiences are gained, but the end product is not what I really wanted. I realized that regardless of the challenges that I face, whether they are personal, professional, financial, or physical, a winning strategy is the key to achieving RESULTS.

When I began to apply some of the qualities I witnessed in my patients—especially their winning attitudes--to my own life, I began to achieve remarkable RESULTS. Not only did I see how a winning formula could help people to overcome a tremendous trauma in their lives, I also recognized its even greater potential in taking on new goals or challenges.

This book is not simply a collection of human-interest stories about people who have overcome the trauma of amputation, nor is it a book written solely for people who have undergone amputation. This book is a manual for creating your own winning strategy for success. Whether you are going to school, playing a sport, building your own business, working as an executive or looking for a new job, this book is about customizing a plan to achieve your RESULTS.

A solid game plan articulates your strategy for success and is the single most important factor in achieving RESULTS. It does not matter how short or long, how simple or detailed your plan is. What is important is recognizing that having a strategy will make the difference between the dream of success and the reality of RESULTS.

RESULTS Strategy

At the end of each chapter, you will find one or more questions that recap the chapter and provide you with the foundation you need to create your own RESULTS strategy. Take a moment to reflect on each question before moving on to the next chapter.

Do you have a specific goal (what are the RESULTS) you want to achieve?

R = RESPONSIBLE to get the job done

E

S

U

L

T

S

Chapter One

Responsible to Get the Job Done

Have you ever noticed that when good things happen, people are quick to take responsibility for the outcome? But when things go wrong, when the problems start to stack up, or when the challenges become overwhelming, no one wants to stand up and say, "I am the one responsible."

President Harry Truman had a sign on his desk in the Oval Office that read "The Buck Stops Here." His attitude exemplified what it means to take responsibility. President Truman understood that even though he may not have started the chain of events or caused the problem, he was clearly willing to stop the litany of excuses and start making solutions.

People who have undergone amputation demonstrate this quality because they cannot escape the obvious fact of amputation. They are the ones now missing a limb and they are the ones who will make the single biggest impact on their recovery. Amputations are often not the result of a catastrophic event; individuals may have developed bone cancer, for example, an event completely beyond their control. However, once the limb is amputated, these people are the ones now facing a significant new challenge. Taking responsibility and accepting that they are the ones who will make the biggest difference in their recovery is key to achieving RESULTS.

Achieving RESULTS means accepting responsibility. If achieving RESULTS is your goal, your dream, and your challenge, then it is your responsibility to get the job done. The initial stage of taking responsibility is found in the root word *respond*. You must acknowledge that the issue at hand is real and that at the very least a physical or mental response is required. At the outset, the response may take the form of pure emotional venting. That's okay, because it's a start. If nothing else, it will wake you up and get your energy flowing. Regardless of the challenges we face, whether they are personal, professional, financial, or physical, a winning strategy can only start to take form when you respond to the situation and initiate some type of positive mental or physical action. I have asked hundreds of patients over the years about their first thoughts or emotions after amputation. The vast majority of their responses reflects two mindsets:

1. Why did this happen to me?
2. What am I going to do?

These responses are instinctive to most of us when we encounter a stressful situation. Yet neither of these responses is overly constructive or empowering. There is no question that reacting to a traumatic or stressful situation with a sense of mourning or loss is human nature. The challenge lies in getting focused on creating a solution (mental action) and on taking the necessary steps (physical action) to act on the solution.

When you are faced with a challenge or hardship, how do you respond? The key to achieving RESULTS is turning two instinctive but passive responses ("why did this happen to me"? and "what am I going to do"?) into active statements: This did happen to me and I am going to do something about it. The response changes from a passive "Why do I have to take on this task and how am I going to do it?" to an active "This is my challenge and I will accomplish my goal." Whether you are going after a new goal or facing a new challenge, accepting the situation and taking responsibility is where the seeds of RESULTS are sown.

One of the first things you can do about the situation is to set a realistic timetable. What is the difference between a dream and a goal? A goal is a dream with a deadline. Think about a goal you are working toward: Does it have a defined timetable and a deadline for achieving it? Without a deadline and a timetable, what you have is a dream. You need to respond to the situation by taking responsibility, by setting a realistic date to accomplish your goal and then starting to work toward creating RESULTS.

There is a proverb that teaches, "The second best time to plant a tree is today; the best time to plant a tree is twenty years ago." All too often we interact with individuals who are playing a waiting game: waiting for the ideal time to quit smoking or to begin a diet or a new exercise routine. This waiting usually has no relevance to the goal at hand. My patients have demonstrated that waiting to make a decision does not help. Once a limb has been amputated, every day counts toward making the commitment to walk again. The question asked by every amputee I have ever worked with is "How long until I can walk again?" Although my answer varies with each case, I always stress that a well-defined timetable should be established before the real work can start.

If your goal is RESULTS, then you need to ask yourself the basic question, When will I achieve my goal? Although the answer may vary according to the size and nature of your goal, the fact remains that you need to ask the question and, more importantly, that you respond to your question before you start your journey toward achieving RESULTS. No one else can address this essential detail. Setting a timetable to achieve your goal is your responsibility.

Responsibility is often confused with doing all the work, but that is not what responsibility is all about. Responsibility means simply putting yourself in the center of the situation or opportunity. You are the one who is required to respond because you are the one who will be most affected by your actions and the actions of those you rely upon. The key here is what your actions will be, what you are going to do.

Depending upon the situation, the first step in being responsible may be admitting that you are in over your head or overwhelmed by the circumstances and that you need help. Some people think that asking for help is a sign of weakness or of passing the buck; that cannot be further from the truth. There are very few examples, if any, of someone achieving greatness or great results without the assistance of others. World-class athletes and Olympic gold medalists may stand on the podium alone, but it took a team of coaches, therapists, mentors, and other support members to enable them to reach their moment of greatness.

Over the years my patients have taught me again and again that the way to achieve RESULTS is to take control, to stay focused, and to seek out the best people. I have treated countless individuals who were told by others "You will never walk again." These same individuals ignored what the "experts" were telling them and instead began searching for the right person to help them get back on their feet again. It is impressive how some individuals choose to stay focused and determined. They choose to reject the negative input, refusing to allow it to cloud their focus or dampen their spirit, and they continue to seek out those who will help them achieve their desired RESULTS.

Think of the times you have shared a dream or goal with friends, family, or work associates only to have them tell you, "You can't do that!" With support like that, your chances of success have to be pretty slim. You need to ask yourself, "Will I allow that person to prevent me from achieving my goal?" If you answer yes, you are destined for failure. You need to answer "NO, I will not allow others to prevent me from achieving my goal!" By doing so, you have just accepted responsibility for your goal and you are on your way to achieving RESULTS.

If the dream or goal is important to you and worth fighting for, you need to take the responsibility to reach out and find individuals who will support you, encourage you, and share your vision. Who will be on your RESULTS team? A co-worker? A family member? A friend? Perhaps the best person to help you achieve your goal is someone you have not even met yet. Creating a winning strategy involves building a winning team…and it is your responsibility to find and surround yourself with supportive people to create your winning team.

I am continually amazed by people who face incredible challenges and who triumph over seemingly insurmountable obstacles to learn how to walk and run again. The foundation for overcoming the challenges lies in the concept of taking responsibility. The ability to ACCEPT the challenge, RESPOND to the situation, and TAKE CONTROL of one's actions is what defines responsibility and sets the stage for achieving RESULTS.

RESULTS Strategy

Have you accepted responsibility for achieving your RESULTS?

How have you "responded" to your situation? Have you taken constructive physical and/or mental action to achieve your RESULTS?

Have you established a realistic timetable to achieve your RESULTS?

Who will be on your team to support you in achieving your RESULTS?

R

E = EXPECTATIONS are clear and concise

S

U

L

T

S

Chapter Two

Expectations Are Clear and Concise

A twelve-year-old girl who had lost her leg to cancer came to my clinic for an evaluation. When I asked her what she wanted to be able to do with her new prosthesis, her answer surprised me. "I can show you," she said with a smile. She took a small book out of a backpack and opened it to a page with two photographs and a small drawing all in a row.

The first picture showed her playing with a friend at the park and was taken a few years before the amputation. Beneath this photo was the caption "Who I Was." The second photo, a recent picture of her in a wheel chair after the amputation, had the caption "Who I Am." The third image on the page, the drawing, was of a little girl running in a field covered with flowers. Its caption read "Who I Will Be." Pointing to the drawing, she looked me in the eye and said, "I want you to help me be the girl in this picture." I had no doubt at that moment that the young lady was destined for a very positive prosthetic experience. She had already grasped an essential concept in overcoming adversity to fulfill a life dream.

Setting clear expectations is a giant step in achieving RESULTS. This establishes your desired outcome, defining exactly what it is you want to achieve. The more specific your goal and the more specific your expectations, the greater the probability of success. In addition, you will be able to communicate your expectations to others more easily and effectively.

It is important to understand that an expectation is not the same as a goal or dream. An expectation is the belief mechanism that turns a goal into reality. It is based upon a positive, focused vision of what you believe is possible and defines your potential and what you imagine to be within your grasp. To expect something is to know in your heart and soul that you will achieve your goal and obtain RESULTS. Many patients over the years have demonstrated the power of setting expectations. It was my children, however, who helped me clarify the concept.

Ask my sons (or any child, for that matter) around Christmas time what their expectations are for the upcoming holiday. They will tell you on which day of the week Christmas falls, why Christmas is celebrated, who is coming to visit them on Christmas Eve, what presents they hope to receive, and what they believe they have to do to deserve the presents they expect to find under the tree. If you have a lot of time on your hands, ask them to elaborate on the presents they are asking for (and feel free to replace "asking for" with "expecting"). Children will provide you with more details about a toy than you ever thought humanly possible. They will describe the color, size, and shape as well as the store they saw it in. Finally, and most importantly, they will tell you what they will do with the toy once they receive it on Christmas morning. Children clearly understand the concept of expectations. Their expectations far exceed the bounds of wishes, dreams, or goals. Children have no doubt that everything they have visualized will in fact take place when Christmas Day arrives.

How do you transform your goal into an expectation? The process begins as a matter of belief. Do you believe your goal is obtainable? It does not matter what others think--do you believe it can be done? Note the question is not whether you can do it, but rather, can it be done? Too often people spend time focusing on themselves and on their doubts about whether they can accomplish a particular goal. Shift the focus to the goal itself. Is the goal realistic and obtainable? Have others accomplished this goal? Once you are convinced that the goal is possible, you have completed the first step toward creating an expectation of success.

The next step is working on creating a strong, unwavering belief in your ability to accomplish the goal by acquiring self-confidence. Ask yourself: With time, effort, learning, and support from others, is it possible for me to achieve this goal? Ask yourself again: Is it possible? Yes, there may be a significant number of factors and circumstances that would first have to be in place, but is it possible? If you can answer at least "Maybe, with time, effort, learning and support from others it will be possible for me to achieve my goal," you have created the beginnings of belief, self-confidence, and expectations.

High expectations are the belief mechanisms that support a goal and give it strength, but low expectations can undermine a goal and make it fade away. Low expectations can stir up two common feelings that will tear apart the best plans and doom them to failure: self-doubt and lack of confidence. I was working with a man who had lost his leg in a farming accident. What was most memorable about his recovery was that although he was doing well and progressing on schedule, he was also extremely discouraged and impatient with learning to walk on his new prosthesis. One day in clinic he was very emotional and short-tempered. He blurted out in a frustrated tone, "I will never get the hang of this in time." "In time?" I asked. "In time for what?" He explained that his daughter was going to be married in two months, and he was worried that he would be unable to walk his daughter down the aisle. I asked him why he thought that. He explained that he could only take small steps, that he still had pain, and that he could not walk without two crutches. Looking at him that day, I could not help but agree. If the wedding were today, he would indeed be unable to walk down the aisle. But the wedding was two months away, and I assured him that in two months he would be doing much better. In my professional opinion, his goal of walking down the aisle was not only realistic but attainable. We agreed that together we would make this our common goal and set our expectations on achieving success in time for the wedding day. I took his chart and wrote on the front of the file in very large letters: Patient will walk his daughter down the aisle on May 24.

It did not take long until every nurse, physician, and therapist in the clinic was aware of this very specific goal. Soon everyone involved with his rehabilitation was supporting the same expectation. He had his wife measure the length of the aisle in the church, and then we marked the floor of the therapy clinic so we all could visualize the exact distance he would have to walk. One of the therapists made the extra effort to teach him how to take steps from side to side so that he would be prepared to dance with his daughter at the reception. The expectation had been identified, visualized, and communicated. The expectation created a change in his attitude, which in turn had a significant impact on this progress and the final RESULTS.

His progress continued at a slow, steady pace, as we had expected. After a few weeks, the only thing that was improving more than his ability to walk was his attitude. His frustration was replaced with excitement. He displayed spirit; his attitude grew increasingly positive. He began to talk about the upcoming day with enthusiasm and while he was in therapy learning how to walk he would hum the melody of the Wedding March. Having a clear expectation of exactly how far he wanted to walk allowed him to set a specific goal and, more importantly, to obtain it. By the time the wedding took place, he might not have been ready to go back to work nor was he yet capable of going for long walks or playing sports. What he was capable of, however, was, in his words, "taking the most important walk of my life" as he escorted his daughter down the aisle.

When the focus is on RESULTS, remember that the "E" in RESULTS does not stand for "Excuses." I have learned this lesson from my patients many times over the years. Someone who has lost both legs and wants to learn to walk again would appear to have two good excuses for not being able to do so. Excuses are not part of solving the issue; they are at the root of the challenge. The tendency to make excuses is the reason why a game plan to achieve RESULTS is needed in the first place.

To achieve RESULTS, it is important to accept the fact that there are no acceptable excuses. I keep a piece of paper in a silver frame over my desk. This paper represents the list of acceptable excuses for not getting the job done. The paper is blank, a constant reminder that whenever I am working on any project, no matter what the pressure, timeline, obstacles or opportunity, the only acceptable excuse I can make to the people I work with must appear on that list. This is not to say that things can't go wrong. But when they do go wrong, excuses won't fix or solve the problem. Wasting time and energy explaining why it wasn't my fault won't fix or solve the problem. What is important is staying focused on getting the job done.

Setting clear and concise expectations creates the foundation for a strong belief, both in yourself and in your goal. By having a strong belief in yourself and in your ability to achieve your goal, you can expect to achieve RESULTS.

RESULTS Strategy

Do you have a clear picture in your mind of exactly what you expect to achieve in your RESULTS?

Have you complete faith, confidence, and belief that your RESULTS can be accomplished?

Do you believe that with time, effort, and learning you can achieve your RESULTS?

Are there any acceptable excuses for not achieving your RESULTS?

R

E

S= SOLUTIONS to manage challenges

U

L

T

S

Chapter Three

Solutions to Manage Challenges

RESULTS start to happen when you get past focusing on the problem and start creating solutions to overcome the challenges. When someone is frustrated or just plain discouraged, we tend to ask, "What's the problem?" Although the spirit and intent of this question may reflect genuine concern and interest, the question nevertheless focuses on the problem and invites further discussion of it: what is wrong, how and when it happened, whose fault it was, and what is holding you back.

As a specialist who designs and fits artificial limbs, I know that one of the most pointless questions you can ask a person lying in a hospital bed following an amputation is "What's the problem?" Everyone would agree the problem is fairly obvious. As participants in life, we all excel at recognizing the problem. The challenge we face is to see the options, to create solutions. I do not mean to suggest that creating solutions is not benefited by a clear understanding and appreciation of all the important aspects of the problem. Being aware of the "who, what, when, where, and why" of the problem or challenge is indeed helpful. If nothing else, you educate yourself about what not to do in the future. But the secret to RESULTS is to visualize the solutions, instead of focusing on the problem.

My patients have a special ability to assess their situation at face value. They must live with something they know they cannot change; they may not want to accept it, but to achieve RESULTS they must find ways around the obstacles. There is no cure for amputation; once a leg has been amputated, it can never grow back. This obvious fact can actually be turned to an advantage by forcing the individual to look at creative solutions. After all, there is no way to "undo" the problem. With the problem so clearly stated, the individual has no choice but to redefine success with new solutions. Addressing new issues, overcoming obstacles, or facing a crisis is much simpler when the solution is tailored to fit a clearly defined challenge.

This concept can be applied to almost any situation in which you are faced with a challenge or hardship. Ask yourself:

Can I fix this problem?

Do I really want to spend time trying to erase the problem or am I better off working to create a solution?

Does it really make any difference whose fault it is? Will assigning blame have any real impact on what I need to do to create a solution?

The point where you can make a difference is when you take your focus away from the problem and shift it to the solution. For example, some people describe themselves as "problem solvers." Once again, where is the focus? It's on the problem. There are many instances, like amputation, where the problem simply cannot be erased. Being a problem solver is okay, but being a "solution solver" is even better...and much more productive.

In creating new solutions, some people rely on the ability to "think outside the box." The whole concept of thinking outside the box has evolved because of our tendency to limit the way we look at and deal with situations. We become set in our ways when addressing difficulties or taking on new challenges. Even if you are one of those people who excel at thinking outside the box, there is still the chance that once you have come up with your good idea, you will quickly jump back into the box to be safe and secure in your familiar comfort zone. I have learned that there are significant benefits to not only think outside the box, but to ask the question "why did I get into the box to begin with"?

Here is a puzzle that will test your ability to think out-side the box. The goal is to connect all nine dots with four straight lines without taking your pencil off the page. It can be done, but there is only one way to do it. The trick is to think outside the box. Give it a try.

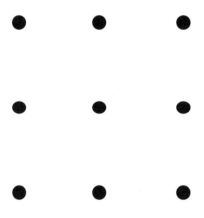

How did you do? The solution is on page 45. As you can see, a solution is possible by going outside the confines of the original "box" of nine dots. It is amazing how many people will struggle with this puzzle and refuse to draw a line outside of the box. Yet nowhere in the instructions are you told that you cannot go outside the area defined by the dots. Most people assume that they are supposed to stay in the defined area. This puzzle is an excellent example of how people can prevent success by limiting their own boundaries.

My patients have demonstrated that it is not only possible to think outside the box, but it is actually fun to live outside the box. I worked with a ninety-five-year-old woman, teaching her stretching and strengthening exercises in preparation for fitting her with a new artificial limb. I remember her telling me, "I never exercised in ninety-five years. Now that I am old and have lost a leg, I get to be a hard body!" That is a perfect example of the mind stepping outside the box! She was doing things that she had never before considered, and her focus had shifted dramatically to new ideas and concepts to achieve RESULTS.

I have seen the potential for this spirit in everyone, from young children to middle-aged men and women to grandmothers and grandfathers. Up until the day they had a leg amputated, many were set in their ways. They were neither prepared for, nor had any control over, this new challenge in their lives. Yet they found it within themselves to look at new ways and new techniques to overcome adversity--not because they wanted to, but because they had no choice. Amputation creates a situation that requires an individual to look at new ways and ideas to overcome new obstacles...to think outside the box. It has become obvious to me that everyone has the ability to focus on solutions and look at new ways to create a positive game plan.

My grandfather was the one who taught me the secret of how to think outside the box. In a striking coincidence during my first year of college to study in prosthetics, my grandfather had a leg amputated due to complications from diabetes. My grandfather and I had always been close, so that his fate seemed like a strange irony that would create yet another tie to strengthen our already close bond. As a World War II veteran, he had many friends who had lost limbs in the war, and he told me that over the years he would often wonder what it was like to be an amputee. He imagined what the struggle, inconvenience, and pain must have been like for his war buddies. About a year after his amputation, Grandpa told me that everything he had imagined, everything he had visualized, was nothing like reality. The one piece of wisdom that always comes to mind whenever I remember Grandpa is "Don't ever try to imagine what it is like to be an amputee because nothing you can imagine will come close."

Until he shared those words with me, I have to admit I often tried to imagine what it would be like to wear an artificial limb. I figured that if I was going to be designing and fitting them for the rest of my career, it only made sense to try to appreciate what it would be like to live with an amputation. Grandpa's words forever changed my mindset and opened my mind to thinking outside the box. His words were a constant reminder that whatever I imagined or conceptualized was limited by the boundaries of my perception--my box, if you will. The only way to create new and innovative ideas and to get out of my box was to ask questions, lots of questions. Whenever I take on a new challenge, the first thing I want to do is ask as many questions as possible. Has this been done before? How can this be done differently? Are there details I have not considered? Are there things I need to learn? Whom do I need to consult?

This concept of thinking outside my box by asking lots of questions not only allowed me to provide better clinical care but quickly had a significant impact on my personal and business decisions as well. By asking questions I found myself being exposed to new ideas and allowing my mind to see new possibilities.

The key to success is to open yourself to new ideas, new concepts and new solutions to maximize your potential. If you are struggling to achieve success, accept the fact that you need to get out of your comfortable little box and stimulate your brain--you need to create a spark to get the ideas going. Stop trying to create a solution all by yourself, and start asking questions of everyone you know, even if they are not familiar with the details. All you need is one spark to light a fire under a new idea or concept. This is the key that will enable you to take a step outside your box and look at the task from a different angle in order to create new and innovative solutions.

Once you have started thinking outside the box by asking questions, you can begin to create your solution. The most overlooked part of creating a great solution is the planning stage, when you build the foundation of your strategy. Too often we get so focused on the final RESULTS and so consumed by the excitement of anticipated success that some of the obvious and essential steps are overlooked or not given sufficient consideration. Having a game plan is essential to achieving your RESULTS.

A game plan satisfies three significant requisites. First, it keeps you on track for success. Second, it provides a series of clear achievement indicators that help you monitor your progress and confirm that you are on the right track. Third, it takes your focus off the problem, which is a negative influence, and keeps your focus on the solution, which is the approach that delivers RESULTS.

The lessons learned from rehabilitation are easily transferred into everyday life. In rehab, a detailed, step-by-step treatment schedule is developed by first asking questions to determine the specific needs, desires, and goals of each patient. Then the appropriate therapists, specialists, and other health care professionals are enlisted to provide the specific services and care required. Most importantly, though, the treatment plan is clearly communicated to all parties involved and a realistic timetable is established to achieve each step of the therapy. Central to this entire process is the patient. The patient is the key to the success of the therapy and is the one who determines the speed with which it moves along. It is critical for the patient to understand and believe in the solution.

Now, let's apply this process to taking on a new goal or overcoming a personal challenge. The formula remains the same:

1. Ask questions; create an environment in which every idea, good or bad, has value because it may be the creative spark for the best solution. Determine the specific needs, desires, and goals to achieve RESULTS.

2. Identify any friends, associates, or family members who can provide assistance in achieving your goal.

3. Communicate your goals clearly to all parties assisting you by sharing your timetable for achieving each step of the plan.

4. Involve yourself in the solution. Remember that you are the axis around which the entire process revolves. You are the one who determines the speed and the success of your RESULTS.

Regardless of what you are going to accomplish, there is incredible power in writing down your solution or plan of action. It doesn't matter if it is full of details, typed with headings and sub-headings, or if it is simply scribbled on the back of a napkin. What is important is that it is written down so that you can refer to it regularly to stay on track. It will remind you what you need to do each day to get another step closer to your RESULTS.

Solution to puzzle on page 37.

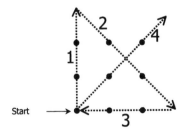

RESULTS Strategy

Do you think outside the box? Have you asked all the questions that can be asked about creating positive RESULTS?

Have you identified everyone who can assist you in achieving your RESULTS?

Have you communicated your goals and expectations to others?

Are you focused on creating a solution to achieve your RESULTS?

Are you actively involved in the process of making your RESULTS a reality?

R

E

S

U = UNDERSTAND the job

L

T

S

Chapter Four

Understand the Job

One of my favorite lines is from the movie Rocky III. Just before his big fight with Rocky Balboa, Clubber Lang is asked by a reporter, "what's your predication for the fight?" Clubber Lang's response was to the point: "I predict pain." Clearly, Clubber Lang had a very good understanding of his job. He recognized and accepted that the job of heavyweight champion of the world involved pain.

I am not suggesting that you must endure pain in order to accomplish a goal or achieve RESULTS. On the contrary, I propose that by achieving a clear and concise understanding of ALL the aspects of the job ahead of you, you may avoid unnecessary pain and stress. More importantly, by accepting ALL the parameters of the job, you will improve your chances of achieving RESULTS.

As the director of a large rehab clinic, I have the responsibility of supervising resident practitioners who are preparing to write certification exams in prosthetics. To qualify to sit for the exams, each resident is required to provide a letter of recommendation from a supervisor. During a performance evaluation with one of the senior residents, I informed him that unless he made a significant improvement in his patient charting and paperwork responsibilities, I would be unwilling to recommend him to sit for the upcoming exams. His response was to attempt to move the focus of my evaluation to his clinical skills and accomplishments. I was in complete agreement with his points. Yes, he was a gifted clinician. Yes, he had exceeded all expectations with regard to evaluating, designing, and fitting high-quality artificial limbs. Then he made a statement that revealed the source of his conflict: "I don't want to become a prosthetist to do great paperwork; I want to become a prosthetist to design and fit great arms and legs." He saw the tasks of clinical care and quality paperwork as being completely unrelated to one another and of unequal importance. He still needed to acquire a complete and clear understanding of ALL aspects of what it took to be a prosthetist.

To achieve RESULTS, it is necessary to acknowledge that there are numerous aspects to every challenge or job. Every aspect of the job becomes a link in the chain, and the strength of the chain depends upon the strength of each link. As the old adage goes, "A chain is only as strong as its weakest link."

Amputees who have learned to walk on an artificial limb demonstrate an understanding of the connection between the work and achieving RESULTS. We can benefit from their example. By evaluating what is required to achieve your ultimate goal, you prepare and equip yourself to address the issues that commonly hold people back from success.

Understanding the job has four benefits:

1. Reduction of stress, anxiety, and fear of the unknown
2. Identification of areas for needed assistance
3. Preparation for potential setbacks
4. Reduction of chances for surprises

One of the most common emotional responses generated by a new challenge is the fear of the unknown. This fear creates anxiety and stress, which in turn drains energy and creates doubt about your ability to achieve RESULTS. When working with people immediately after they have undergone amputation, the level of stress, anxiety, and fear of the unknown is significant. In some instances, the fear of the unknown is more devastating than the reality of the amputation itself. One of the most effective methods for addressing this fear is to introduce recent amputees to individuals who have successfully completed prosthetic rehabilitation and are now enjoying active lifestyles. Meeting others who have experienced what they themselves are now going through not only reduces anxiety and relieves some stress but also allows the individual to ask questions and get answers regarding "the unknown."

When you take on a new challenge or are faced with a crisis, how often do you get that uneasy feeling in your stomach? Your mind starts to work overtime and your stress and anxiety levels build to a point where all aspects of your life are affected. Before you get to this point, you need to respond to the situation and take action by seeking out someone who has been in the same situation before. Step outside your box and ask questions. Regardless of what you are attempting to accomplish or what you are up against, someone somewhere has been in a similar situation. If that person is still around, he or she must have survived the ordeal and are probably willing to share the victory with you. By seeking out others who have achieved success before you, you can eliminate the fear of the unknown, because now you will know what to expect.

As you start to learn what to expect, you will acquire another advantage–understanding the job–which will help you identify areas where you may require assistance. When taking on a new goal, it is important to inventory your strengths, but more importantly, to identify areas that may need improvement or special attention. People often refer to these areas as weaknesses, but I have learned that they are weaknesses only if you ignore them or don't acknowledge your need to grow. As soon as you identify an area where you need to grow, change, or improve, that area can now actually be considered a strength, because you have recognized your need to take action to achieve RESULTS.

Unfortunately, if you're like most people, the things that need improvement are usually the very things we don't like to do and don't want to deal with. It is important to recognize the crucial relationship between achieving your goal and being willing to deal with all aspects of the job. Remember the resident who did not like doing paperwork in his job as a practitioner. When it comes to achieving RESULTS it is important to recognize that you do not do a good job unless you do the whole job.

There is significant benefit in asking yourself what part of the job you like the least, what frustrates you the most and causes you the most stress. Once you answer that, you have the part you need to work on the most, because it is part of the whole job. Your success and ability to achieve RESULTS depends upon your ability to do all parts of the job.

Knowing your strengths and any areas that could stand improvement prepares you for potential set-backs. As you work toward your goal, it is important to recognize that certain aspects of the job may be more difficult or require more effort than you had expected. You will also need to understand that certain steps along the way may be beyond your immediate control. If you experience a setback, the most damaging impact is typically a significant amount of frustration and anxiety, creating doubt about achieving

RESULTS. By making an effort to identify and understand the potential challenges that could interfere with the pursuit of your goal, you will effectively prepare yourself for mishaps. By being aware that a particular setback is a possibility, the level of doubt and anxiety will subside, allowing you to maintain faith and belief in your ability to achieve RESULTS. Furthermore, you will learn that most setbacks do not destroy goals; they just delay them.

Understanding the job also reduces the element of surprise. Having an understanding and appreciation of all the details in pursuit of your goal eliminates the chance of the "unexpected" happening. In most instances, what is unexpected is really something that has been glossed over or not considered in the planning stages. People are incorrect when they refer to a pregnancy or a bill as "unexpected." Either of these situations is foreseeable to some degree and is likely to be based upon actions of the very people involved. Don't be caught offguard; prepare yourself to deal with any challenges or "unexpected" surprises by understanding all the steps along your path to success.

As you begin to understand the job and identify what is required to reach your goal, it is important to avoid becoming overwhelmed or discouraged. Any new job will be hard before it becomes easy. Understanding the job and recognizing those areas where you will be challenged demonstrates maturity and responsibility. Understanding the job empowers and prepares you to pursue and achieve RESULTS.

RESULTS Strategy

Are there any aspects of the tasks involved in obtaining your RESULTS that you don't understand or are concerned about? Do you know someone who has successfully completed those tasks? Have you asked them about your concerns?

Have you identified aspects of the tasks that you do not like to do or deal with? Are you taking steps to become more effective in addressing any areas that require improvement?

Are you prepared to deal with any setbacks or "unexpected" situations?

R

E

S

U

L = LEARN what you need to know

T

S

Chapter Five

Learn What You Need to Know

Children have inquisitive minds. They soak up knowledge like sponges and continually ask questions. Why is the sky blue and the grass green? Does chocolate milk come from brown cows? Are we there yet? This curiosity is especially evident when a child takes on a new project. Immediately, the questions start. Whatever the situation, the child wants to know more. Unfortunately, this instinctive quest for learning seems to come to an end as we age.

Somewhere in our teens, the insatiable quest for learning seems to shift to a desire to be right; asking questions and admitting "I don't know" seem to represent some sign of weakness. I have observed that people who take on new situations often implement something I call the S.W.A.G. Principle. You may never have heard of it, but you have undoubtedly seen it applied by others if you haven't applied it yourself many times. People apply the S.W.A.G. Principle when they find themselves in a new situation or taking on a new challenge. Deep down inside, they know that they have never done anything like this before, so they eventually do what comes naturally: They make a Scientific Wild Ass Guess.

Does any of this sound familiar? Maybe you have been pretty sure about what to do. Perhaps you have already been in a situation like the one you're in now, only it was a little different. Perhaps you believe your real-life experiences have prepared you to take on any new challenge in life. The S.W.A.G. Principle worked before, right?

Try to imagine the situation the majority of my patients face after amputation. Consider the seventy-seven-year-old person about to have a limb amputated because of diabetes. Assuming this person probably learned to walk around the age of two, he has been walking for a total of seventy-five years. And like anyone with two good legs, he tends to take the art of walking pretty much for granted. How about you? Every morning you wake up, swing your feet out of bed, and away you go. No thought process, no complicated calculations, no real skill or experience required–you just walk. Right?

Now I ask you, how much help will the seventy-five years of walking experience be to the person the day after amputation? The answer is NONE. No assistance at all. The seventy-five years of walking experience is of no real value now. Once a leg has been amputated, walking becomes a whole new challenge. So much for everything you ever knew, or thought you knew, about walking. You need to learn to walk using a method and technology you probably know nothing about. It's time to start all over again.

Does it not stand to reason that if you take on a new task or challenge in your life or do anything you have never done before, that maybe, just maybe, you might need to learn something new before you can be successful? Every amputee with whom I have ever worked has figured out this concept very quickly and used it to his or her advantage. Regardless of age or background, someone who has just had an amputation recognizes the need to learn new concepts and new techniques if he or she is ever going to walk again. The ability to identify the need to learn and to admit "I don't know" is a powerful tool in achieving RESULTS.

I believe that when we are born we are given two invisible buckets that we carry with us for the rest of our lives. These two buckets contain the knowledge that we have acquired or will acquire and, more importantly, retain in our lifetime. One bucket is labeled STUFF I KNOW THAT I KNOW. This bucket contains the information and experience you have acquired over the years. You have no doubt about knowing the stuff that is in this bucket. When I look in my own STUFF I KNOW THAT I KNOW bucket, I see the basics of prosthetics as well as how to drive a car, how to make my children laugh, how to mow my lawn, how to play soccer. This bucket is the one I use every day because it contains the stuff that I know I know.

The other invisible bucket we carry around is labeled STUFF I KNOW THAT I DON'T KNOW. If you are like most people, this bucket will be considerably larger than the other one. When I look in my own STUFF I KNOW THAT I DON'T KNOW bucket, I see the Chinese language. Over one billion people on this planet speak the Chinese language, but I am not one of them. There's lots of other stuff in that bucket, stuff like quantum physics, aerospace engineering, the new tax code and where the dryer hides my sock.

There is much to learn and appreciate about these two buckets. They are always with us. We can put more "know" into the first bucket and remove some "don't know" from the second any time we choose. Knowledge can fall out of the buckets at any time as well. We can trade our buckets for larger or smaller ones, but the important thing about these buckets is that you have sole control over absolutely everything that goes in, or falls out of, your bucket.

Every time you take on a new challenge or start a new task, you should stop and take a moment to look deep inside your buckets. Make sure that what you need to know is in one of them. If you find what you are looking for, then stop and identify the bucket you found it in. If the knowledge you need to rely upon is in the bucket labeled STUFF I KNOW I DON'T KNOW, this is not time to start using the SWAG principle, you definitely need to start learning. Start looking in other people's buckets, read a book, do some research, ask some questions, do whatever you need to do. But before you take on the new challenge, make sure you do everything in your power to confirm that the knowledge or experience you require is firmly packed into your STUFF I KNOW THAT I KNOW bucket.

Our two invisible buckets also hold something that may be more valuable than knowledge, and that's ATTITUDE. In some circumstances it is more important to learn a new attitude than a new ability. The right attitude clarifies your thinking and enables you to recognize the skills or talents you need to learn.

A six-year-old boy brought this home to me. He had lost his leg in an accident. One Saturday morning his father was cutting the grass on a riding lawn mower when he asked his son to get him a soda from the house. The little boy ran into the house, his mother gave him a soda, and the boy hurried back out to deliver the soda to his father. In his excitement he ran toward the lawn mower and tripped. He slid under the mower, and in an instant his right foot was gone.

I met with the family one month after the accident to fit the young boy with his first prosthesis. What I remember most about working with this family was the heavy cloud of guilt and depression that engulfed them. The parents carried the full weight of responsibility squarely on their shoulders, and they openly shared their grief. Dad had wanted a soda, Mom had given their son the soda, and now their son would be missing a foot for the rest of his life. In the midst of all this guilt was the little boy. For the first few weeks I remember him as being very quiet, very sad, and harboring his own sense of guilt. He knew it was because of his tripping that everyone was so sad.

All of this changed some time later when I was casting him for a new prosthesis. Just like other growing children who need new pants, shirts, and shoes, he needed a new artificial limb to keep up with his growth spurts. The boy's parents were in the reception area doing some paperwork, making this the first time I had really been with him alone, just the two of us. During the casting he looked at me and said, "Everyone sure is sad because I lost my foot." I told him that it was pretty normal for people to be sad, but that it was because they cared for him so much. Then he asked a question that stopped me cold. "Do you know where my foot is? Maybe if we could find it, everyone would not be so sad." It does not happen often for me, but I was truly at a loss for words. Here was a little boy who honestly believed that his foot was lost, as if he had lost a bike or a toy, and that if he could find it, everyone around him would be happy again. After thinking about his question, I gave him the most mature and intelligent answer I could muster: "I don't know, where do you think it is?" He continued to ask questions, and I continued to respond by turning the questions back to him. The young boy then told me about his grandmother passing away a year earlier and how everyone was sad after that happened, just like they were sad now.

After the casting was finished, I escorted my patient back to his parents. As I opened the door to the reception area, he smiled and announced loudly to his parents, "You don't need to be sad anymore. My foot isn't lost anymore. I know where it is." With a confused look on his face, his father asked him to explain. The answer instantly changed the attitudes of everyone in the room. The little boy said, "My foot is not lost. It is in heaven with Grandma."

`It was incredible how the change in perception of this six-year-old boy could have such a dramatic impact on a group of knowledgeable, responsible, and well-meaning adults. In the middle of all the guilt was this little boy just wanting to get on with things, regain his childhood, and have some fun. What was holding him back was not losing a foot but rather the attitude of everyone around him. His revelation of where the foot was woke everyone up. It provided the spark that the family needed to accept the truth about something that had happened that they could not change. Acceptance and a positive attitude left the I DON'T KNOW bucket and moved over into the I KNOW bucket, letting the family focus on making the best of the situation.

Acknowledge that you may need to learn something new to obtain something new. Wherever you go, whatever you do, remember that you are carrying two invisible buckets with you. These buckets hold the tools and resources you require for taking on new challenges to achieve success. Whether it is knowledge, experience, people skills, self-esteem, confidence, financial management skills, self-discipline, attitude, or whatever you may need for success, check to make sure that you have what you need in your buckets. Embrace learning and you will be one step closer to achieving RESULTS.

RESULTS Strategy

Do you know everything you need to know to achieve success and accomplish your RESULTS?

Do you need to acquire knowledge or, a new skill or attitude to ensure success?

R

E

S

U

L

T = TENACITY to never give up

S

Chapter Six

Tenacity to Never Give Up

As children we all heard the story "The Little Engine That Could" about the littlest train engine that taught us the difference between "I think I can" and "I know I can." At one time or another most of us have offered this advice to a friend who was discouraged: Don't give up, you can do it. Perhaps you have even muttered these words to yourself to get the extra little push you needed to finish a difficult task. Saying the words "Don't give up" is easy, but most will agree the actual act of not giving up is the real challenge--a lot easier said than done.

I was sure I knew what tenacity was when I was a teenager. I firmly believed that I understood what it took to never give up and to have a "keep trying, you can do it" attitude. This belief, however, came to a sudden stop the day I started my residency. I met a twenty-five-year-old man who had lost both arms and one leg in an electrical accident. He was small, frail, and dependent on others for everything. One morning after a casting for one of his arms, I was instructed by the clinical director to push the patient in his wheel chair back to his room. As we started down the hallway, the patient asked me to stop pushing because he wanted to get to his room by himself. He told me that he was going to have to learn to get around on his own someday and that now was a good time to start. I explained that it was hospital policy for all patients to be accompanied on the floor at all times and that I could not let him go by himself. He answered, "Fine, you can stay with me but just don't help." For the next hour we inched along the long corridor as he moved the wheel chair forward one tiny step at a time with his one leg.

I was awestruck by the determination and drive he

demonstrated in accomplishing the task of getting himself to his room under his own power. At any time he could have asked for help, and it would have been so easy for him to give up. I spent the entire time telling him that he had gone far enough on his own and that I could push him the rest of the way. I explained that I needed to get back to the clinic because my boss would wonder where I was and that I did not have time to be escorting him down the hallway at a snail's pace. I also suggested that this was a little too much exercise for him so soon after the accident. All of this was to no avail. He had in his mind what he was going to accomplish and he was going to stick to it until he achieved his goal.

That day I caught my first glimpse of what constitutes real tenacity. Since then I have witnessed hundreds of amputees demonstrating that this powerful "never give up" quality can make the difference between "almost" and success. Most importantly, I learned that the drive and determination to stick to your dream is not something you magically acquire or are born with, but rather it is a talent and a skill that can be learned. There are two fundamentals in learning tenacity as you work toward your goal:

1. Have a purpose.
2. Believe in your goal.

Purpose creates a clear reason for your efforts and is a powerful motivator to keep you focused, determined, and driven in pursuit of your goal.

For one of my co-workers, having a purpose made the difference between walking and a wheel chair. I shared an office with him for over a year. He was a Vietnam vet who had lost one leg above the knee and severely damaged the other in a land mine explosion. One day I asked my friend what it was like for him during his recovery from the accident. He shared with me that for the first year he was confined to either a hospital bed or a wheel chair. After a year of extensive rehabilitation he was told he would most likely never walk again. He told me that the news about not being able to walk again was not what had hit him the hardest. What was devastating was the prospect of being confined to a wheel chair where he would spend the rest of his life literally looking up at people and having them look down at him. At that moment he made a commitment to work toward a single purpose. Every day he would wake up and say to himself, "This will be the day I stand up on two good feet and look at the world eye to eye." This single thought, this single goal, this very specific purpose is what empowered him to achieve his goal and walk out of the hospital on two good feet.

Having a purpose is essential in centering your energy and maintaining your enthusiasm when times get rough. It's a matter of looking closely at your goal and determining the true reason you want to achieve RESULTS. The more specific you are in identifying your purpose, the greater the chance of achieving your goal, because you have created the reason you need and deserve to achieve success. By creating the reason for your efforts, purpose empowers you with the tenacity to achieve RESULTS.

Belief in your goal is another powerful source of

tenacity. Although I have seen many patients demonstrate the effectiveness of a strong belief in achieving RESULTS, it was a close companion of mine that showed me the power of belief. For the past nine years I have had the pleasure of sharing my home with a very likable Dalmatian by the name of Pepper. She has provided me with a daily demonstration of what belief and tenacity are all about. I still remember the first day Pepper came into our home as an excitable little puppy. She had been in her new home for a few hours when someone rang the doorbell. The first one to the door was Pepper, wagging her tail and barking, obviously eager to greet the visitor. Over the past nine years, this scenario has been repeated every single time anyone has ever come to our home and rung the doorbell or knocked on the door. The first one there is always Pepper, showing the same level of excitement and joy over every visitor at the front door. And yet not once has the visitor at the front door ever been for her. Now that's tenacity! Pepper demonstrates an honest belief that someday the knock at the door will be for her, and she wants to make sure that she is there and ready when that day comes.

Having a strong belief in your goal keeps you focused, sustains your ability to be positive, and creates the drive to achieve tenacity. However, you do not want to focus all of your energy on the final prize. Staying completely focused and driving continually toward your final goal or RESULTS can lull you into a false sense of accomplishment. You start believing you are actually doing something when in fact you are expending your energy on VISUALIZING the results rather than WORKING for them. It is important to focus on both, keeping in mind that they are very different concepts.

Visualizing is a valuable tool to motivate and inspire you to stay on track when the going gets tough. It is vital to maintain a clear picture in your mind of what you are working toward and why it is so important for you to succeed. The key to success, however, is using this vision of success to do the work necessary to achieve your goal. Tenacity is the key to DOING what needs to be done.

Thinking, dreaming, visualizing, imagining, planning, preparing, and hoping provide the warm, feel-good sensations to keep you on track. It is when you go to the next step and use these emotions to empower yourself with tenacity that you stay committed to your goal and do the necessary work to make RESULTS a reality.

RESULTS Strategy

What is the single most important reason you want to achieve your RESULTS?

What are you doing on a consistent basis to keep yourself working toward achieving your RESULTS?

R

E

S

U

L

T

S = SIMPLIFY your strategy

Chapter Seven

Simplify Your Strategy

A newborn infant enters a world of simplicity. No worries, no stress, no uncertainties. Life is simple. What I find amazing about the human race is that even though we are all born into a life of simplicity, we tend to "die due to complications." It has always puzzled me why we seem to have a talent for making situations, circumstances, and life complicated.

Do you remember the last time you were faced with a new challenge or were trying to overcome a hardship? If you are like most people, much of the stress you experienced did not come from the notion of the task itself but rather from the details and deadlines associated with the task. You no doubt had to deal additionally with a host of other projects, people, and "stuff" going on in your life. All in all, you faced a fairly involved and detailed set of circumstances. If you were asked to explain the situation, you would probably have used the term most people use when describing challenges: "It's complicated."

Whenever I hear the word "complicated," I immediately think of a young woman I worked with who had lost a leg above the knee and had the other leg partially paralyzed in a hit-and-run accident. To provide care for this patient I had to work closely with a certified orthotist whose job was to design and fit a custom brace that would support the woman's paralyzed leg. After many weeks of exercise, preparation, and planning, the big day came for her to take her first steps. It took a while to position the brace properly on her leg and then to fit the prosthesis on her residual limb. The orthotist and I then assisted her up to her feet and stood her between a set of walking rails. I reviewed the procedure and body movements for taking the first steps with the prosthesis while my associate demonstrated how to walk with the brace. She listened intently, asked no questions, and then, holding on to the railings, took her first step, then another, until she had walked the entire length of the walking rails, turned around, and walked back. Astonished by her accomplishment and the confidence she had demonstrated, I asked her, "You were fantastic, what's your secret?" She looked at me and replied with a huge smile, "I put one foot in front of the other." She had looked past the details, the difficulties, and the complications and had focused on the basics. She had taken the final step in achieving RESULTS, applying a strategy that was simple and directly focused on her expectation of being able to walk.

I do not mean to suggest that details are not important or that challenges are never complicated. However, it is important to look beyond the details and the obstacles in order to develop and implement a strategy to overcome the challenges. Too often people focus all their energy on the details and special circumstances in an attempt to make sure that everything is thought out and prepared for and that the timing is right before they will begin. What needs to be done is making a simple, straightforward plan for achieving success...and then committing to getting the job done.

The NBA playoffs provide an excellent example of this concept. The advertisements for the post-season play say it all: "Win or go home." Simple, direct, and to the point. Every team's bottom-line strategy going into the playoffs is to win; everything else is secondary. The game plan, the coaching, the specific plays are all details, essential to success, but the bottom line is they simply support the main goal: to win. This simple strategy is what makes the playoffs so exciting and is the key to pushing players to their peak performance. Everything they have worked for all season is on the line. Every player has no choice but to stay focused on a very simple yet powerful strategy: win the game.

It is this focus that gives people who have survived amputation a significant advantage when taking on the challenge of learning to stand and walk. For them, they are facing their own personal world championship. Everything is on the line and they are the team captain.

There may be many complications, details, and extenuating circumstances to take into consideration, but achieving success requires the strategy be simple and straightforward, inspired by and focused on the final RESULTS, learning how to stand and walk.

It would be great if we could all carry around our own scoreboard to use on a day-to-day basis. If you became frustrated or overwhelmed, or if you became overly focused on details and complications, you could check the score, an instantaneous reminder to get back on track and stay focused on your strategy: win the game.

Unfortunately there is no magic scoreboard to follow us around, but that is not to say you cannot create a scoreboard of your own to help you stay on track to success. The simplest method is to create a visual reference that you can look at daily or even more often to continually remind you of your goal. It does not matter if it is a simple picture to stick onto your refrigerator, a small written note that you keep in your wallet or an elaborate poster you frame and hang in your office.

The quality and amount of detail is not important; what does count is having a constant reminder and image of exactly what it is you are working toward.

This visual aid also serves as an excellent starting point for taking on a new goal or a new challenge. The first thing to do is ask yourself: "What do I need to DO to get the RESULTS I want?" The answer to this question becomes your bottom-line, simplified strategy. Your strategy should be focused on the specific ACTIONS necessary to achieve success. Next, determine the supporting details to support your action strategy:

1. When will I complete the task?
2. Whose assistance will I need?
3. How do I need to change to achieve success?

The last detail is without a doubt the most difficult one to address. In order to accomplish something new or different, change is not only important, but it should be an essential part of your strategy. There is an old adage that goes, "If you keep doing things the same way you've done them, you will keep getting the same things you've got." I often hear people say, "I don't like change." My reply is always, "Name any moment in the recorded history of man when there has not been change." Think about it: The only true sign of life is change. Without change, everything would remain the same...forever! Change is essential, certainly in obtaining RESULTS. What you are seeking is a different outcome, which by definition means change. If you want to experience change in your life or in your circumstances, then you must change the way you are doing things.

Your strategy for success is based upon your ability to set clear expectations and then to decide exactly what you are willing to DO to achieve them. Decide what you are willing to change in your actions or in your attitude, and start WORKING toward your RESULTS.

RESULTS Strategy

What is the visual reminder you rely upon to keep you focused on your RESULTS?

What actions must you take, what exactly do you need to do to achieve your RESULTS?

Can you complete the following statements that will define your simplified strategy?

1. I will achieve my RESULTS by_____.

2. I will require assistance from _____.

3. To achieve success, I need to change my _____.

R = RESPONSIBLE to get the job done

E = EXPECTATIONS are clear and concise

S = SOLUTIONS to challenges

U = UNDERSTAND the job

L = LEARN what you need to know

T = TENACITY to never give up

S = SIMPLIFY your strategy

Conclusion

About three months into my residency, I was called into the office by my supervisor. He asked me how I thought I was doing. Not being shy, I told him I thought I was doing very well. He then asked me if I thought I would be a good prosthetist. Again, I did not hold back, telling him I would make a great prosthetist. He then became very somber, looked me right in the eye, and said, "Dale, I truly do not believe you will be a very good practitioner, but I believe the person you have the ability to become will do very well." At first, the wisdom of his words escaped me. My ego had gotten stuck on the first part of his sentence. It took me a while to fully appreciate the message he was conveying, but over time it slowly sank in and then made perfect sense.

There was no doubt in my mind that I had the skill, attitude, and ability to do that job; furthermore, I truly loved what I was doing. But I so much wanted to do well, to have the right answers and do everything perfectly that I was not allowing myself to see, hear, and learn what was going on around me. I was so set on making a name for myself by being the best practitioner in the clinic that I was limiting my own growth by defining myself according to who I was that day, not according to who I could be.

Not long after that meeting I began working with a young lady whose arm had been amputated in a work-related accident. She had just come from the Department of Motor Vehicles and was objecting to her classification on her driver's license as "disabled." Sitting in the chair with one arm missing just above what used to be her elbow she looked at me in frustration and asked, "Do I look disabled to you?" She was furious that someone had labeled her based solely upon her present condition. She knew that her inability to do certain things today was temporary and that with time the loss of an arm would become, in her words, "an inconvenience."

How often do we define ourselves or predict our ability to achieve success based upon who we are or what our abilities are at that particular moment? How often do we predict our future, or even worse, allow others to predict our future and our potential based upon our present skills and talents? Perhaps a much better predictor of the RESULTS we are all capable of achieving would be our growth potential and who or what we have the ability to become.

This concept is with me every day as I interact with people who have undergone amputation. The person that I meet in a hospital bed or in a wheelchair will not, at that moment in time, walk or run very well, but that person will grow and achieve significant goals by learning to overcome enormous obstacles. In each evaluation we discuss the expectations and potential outcome of the individual. It's a matter of looking past the apparent challenges, accepting what is and looking forward to what can be. The silver lining of amputation, if there is one, is that the challenges are clear and apparent and that assistance, growth, change, and work are all essential to success; they are not topics for negotiation. Witnessing this kind of growth on a daily basis has served as one of the most valuable tools in my own personal and professional growth.

I have learned to extend this vision to almost every aspect of my life. Whenever I take on a new opportunity, teach my child, work with a friend or face a crisis, I know that at that moment in time, I may not have everything I need to achieve success. I may not yet be the person I need to be to achieve success. By discussing my expectations and visualizing the outcome, I can look past the apparent challenges and see my potential for success. When we learn to accept assistance, growth, change, and work as essential elements of success, we are one step closer to RESULTS.

Creating a RESULTS-focused approach will make a significant impact on your willingness and ability to take on new challenges and opportunities. It will prepare you to address life with a fresh attitude and enthusiasm. Why you are facing a particular challenge and whose fault it is will no longer be relevant. Success starts deep within you. It begins with the thought that you can in fact accept a challenge and overcome any obstacle to become an agent of change. Once you start to think it, you create the foundation to believe it. The next step is to move from belief to action and to implement a RESULTS-focused plan to achieve success.

Devising solutions and a strategy to achieve RESULTS is what will make the most significant impact on success. When you make the choice to focus on RESULTS by creating an action plan for success, you give yourself the chance to stand up one day on two good feet and look life's challenges in the eye, because with RESULTS, There's No Such Word as Can't.

About the Author

Results Coach™ Dale Berry is the President of Dale Berry Presents, a company dedicated to helping people and companies create and implement RESULTS focused strategies to achieve personal and professional goals. With a well-earned reputation as a dynamic and informative presenter, Dale is a highly sought-after lecturer and has been featured as a keynote speaker at meetings in Europe, Canada, Asia and the United States.

Dale is also a practicing Certified Prothetist with over 20 years experience of providing high level reha- bilitative care for amputees around the world. His clinical experiences include being a staff prosthetist in a rehabilitation hospital, Director of Education for a German manufacturing company, Marketing Vice President for a French distribution firm and is presently Vice President of Clinical Operations for the largest rehabilitation company in the world with over 600 facilities nationwide. Dale graduated from George Brown College in Toronto, Canada in 1980 and obtained his Canadian certification in prosthetics in 1983, and in 1992 became certified in the United States. Dale immigrated to the United States in 1986 and now lives in Minneapolis, Minnesota with his wife, two sons and two dogs.

Two Ways to Get RESULTS for Your Business or Organization

1. Invite Dale Berry to Speak at Your Group's Next Gathering
If you enjoyed reading this book, you will want see and hear about achieving RESULTS and experience the dynamic and entertaining message from Results Coach™, Dale Berry. Dale is an entertaining professional public speaker and consultant to individuals and companies in need of creating RESULTS.

If you would like information on having Dale Berry deliver a personalized message at your organization's meeting or event, call or write to the address below.

2. Give Everyone in Your Organization a Copy of This Book
Quantity discounts make this book a valuable business tool you can afford to give your meeting attendees, your staff, and your leadership. . to create a team that consistently delivers RESULTS. Audio, video and motivational items also available.

To book Dale Berry for your next event, and/or to order RESULTS resources in quantity, call or write:

> **Dale Berry Presents**
> **9637 Anderson Lakes Pkwy, #129**
> **Eden Prairie, MN 55344-4155**
> **(952) 943-9472**

Or contact Dale on the Internet at <u>www.ResultsCoach.org</u>
E-mail: Dale@ResultsCoach.org

RAVE PRESENTATION REVIEWS!

"My advice to a company looking for a great speaker is to hire this guy. Dale is terrific, he is a dynamic speaker, he is very believable and is someone who will inspire everyone in your company."

Stuart Bear, Attorney-at-law
Chestnut & Cambronne, Minneapolis, MN

" Dale Berry is a powerhouse. My time is extremely valuable, and attending his presentation was well worth the investment. He delivers an exciting message that gave me specific tools to enhance both my professional career and my personal relationships. My clients expect RESULTS, and Dale's systematic program makes delivering those results a sure thing."

Larry Kriesmer, CLU, Chartered Financial Consultant,
Rancho Santa Fe, CA

Would you like to be included in RESULTS teaching materials?

Have you accomplished something that makes you proud that you made the effort to achieve your goal? Maybe it was a big goal, or perhaps it was a very small achievement that made a big difference to you. I want to hear your stories and learn what it was that made a difference for you to achieve success and deliver bottom-line RESULTS. When you use one of the concepts or principles in this book, please write to me and tell me how it worked for you, and I will make every effort to use your experiences in teaching others. Please include your name so I can properly acknowledge your contribution and include your address and phone number so I can contact you directly if needed.

Please write to me with your RESULTS inspired story at:

Dale Berry Presents
9637 Anderson Lakes Pkwy, #129
Eden Prairie, MN 55344-4155
(952) 943-9472

Or submit your story on our website at www.ResultsCoach.org

Or send me an e-mail at Dale@ResultsCoach.org

FREE STUFF!
Posters, E-Zine, Prosthetic News and RESULTS!

All at

www.ResultsCoach.org

Visit Dale's Website and get RESULTS!

Δ   Find out how you can get a free RESULTS e-poster

Δ   Sign up for Dale's Free E-Zine

Δ   Read how others have created RESULTS

Δ   Add your experiences in creating your own RESULTS

Δ   Nominate yourself or someone else for RESULTS person of the month

Δ   Visit Dale's on-line store and buy his latest books, audios, videos, and RESULTS resources

Δ   Get a Press Kit

Δ   Find out what's new in prosthetics

Δ   Request Dale to speak at your next event

E-mail Dale at Dale@ResultsCoach.org